# Knitting for Children

## A Second Book

*by*

# Bonnie Gosse *and* Jill Allerton

*with photography by* Bonnie Gosse

# Wynstones Press

## By the same authors:

A First Book of Knitting for Children,
published by Wynstones Press.

## Dedications:

*Jill Allerton:*
For the Vancouver Waldorf School community of children, parents and staff who were an important part of my life for 23 years.

*Bonnie Gosse:*
For my parents Lorna and Warren Linklater

## Acknowledgements:

Thank you to Noelani and Michael Dubeta who brought the original leaping cat to share with Jill.

Thank you to Sister Magdalena of Klöster Notersegg in St. Gallen, Switzerland for allowing us to include her lovely leaping cat in our book.

Thank you to Patti Bosomworth who, many years ago, knitted the first 'Lily the Lamb' to help in Class 1.

Thank you to Ingrid Schinkel for the original horned owl.

Thank you to Judy LeCompt for the original 'Baby Running Shoes' as a gift 22 years ago to Bonnie's new baby.

Thank you to Teresa and Alana MacIntosh for all their help.

# Contents

# Abbreviations

| | |
|---|---|
| k | knit |
| p | purl |
| sts | stitches |
| pr | pair |
| ss | stocking stitch (1 row k, 1 row p) |
| cm | centimetres |
| in | inches |
| gm | grams |
| beg. | beginning |
| inc | increase |
| m1 | make 1 stitch |
| psso | pass slipped stitch over |
| sl | slip a stitch |
| dec | decrease |
| tog | together |
| mc | main colour of yarn |
| cc | contrasting colour of yarn |
| tw | twist |
| rib | ribbing |
| * to * | means follow the directions from the first * to the second * |
| yo | yarn over (you will use this to make "proper holes") |

# List of colour illustrations

# Introduction

*Greetings!* Hello again to those of you whom we have met in *A First Book of Knitting for Children*. We hope you have enjoyed learning to knit and that you have made some of the projects in our first book. Welcome to new readers. This book is for those of you who know the basic skills of knitting.

In *A First Book of Knitting for Children* we introduced you to basic knit and purl stitch. We explained some of the problems which can occur, and brought simple patterns, like the Striped Ball, together with more complicated designs using both types of stitch, such as the Cat or the Mother Sea Otter.

In this book we are widening your knitting horizons in several ways. Firstly, we are including many more patterns for you to knit – some have been made in grades three to five in the Vancouver Waldorf School for many years while others are brand new. Secondly, we are introducing you to the way in which commercial patterns are written, so that in the future you can follow one yourself, though in our patterns we are giving more detailed instructions than a commercial pattern does. Sometimes we are quite chatty with the help which we think you may need, so we may sound just as if we are actually there, talking to you! Lastly we are giving you a little bit of guidance with choosing yarn and needles so that your work will turn out successfully.

We sincerely hope that you will become good knitters and retain the skill and the interest, so that you will love this relaxing pastime all your lives, and see your children and grandchildren do the same, as we have done.

## Yarns and needles

Hand knitting has become so popular! Every year more and more people are enjoying both the making and the using or wearing of hand knitted items and garments. This increase in popularity has made the knitting market place grow. Companies that produce yarn have

# Yarns and needles

worked hard to develop new and exciting yarns to capture the interest of knitters. There is now a huge variety of yarns to choose from. Differences in yarns are created in three ways – the fibre used, the amount of fibre used and the method of construction.

Yarn varies in colour, weight (thickness), elasticity, texture, strength and durability. Each yarn will have advantages and disadvantages. In order for a project to turn out successfully you must choose a yarn that is suited to that project, for example using mohair yarn for the froggie would not produce a successful project. The knitting would be too holey, the beans would fall out, and the fussiness of the yarn would hide some of the shaping of the toes and 'fingers'.

For most of our projects we have chosen yarns of natural fibre content – wool, or cotton, because we love the feel of natural fibre yarns. But, for the baby running shoes project we chose a yarn of a man made fibre content, an acrylic yarn, because it washes so easily.

For all of our projects we have chosen smooth, 'plain' yarns as opposed to 'fancy' yarns. Smooth yarns are easier to work with and show up the shaping of a project. Some 'fancy' yarns have loops or fuzz, others have sequins attached or gold or silver thread woven in. The shape or patterning of a project that calls for 'fancy' yarn is often very simple, as the focus of the project is usually the image created by the effects in the 'fancy' yarn, such as fuzz, loops, sequins, gold or silver thread.

It is very important that the correct weight of yarn is used for each project. Some projects will only be successful with a certain weight of yarn while others, such as some in this book, can be worked with either thinner or thicker yarn. A thinner yarn will of course produce a smaller project. It is also very, very important that the size of needles used for a project matches the weight (thickness) of the yarn. The suggested weight of yarn and size of needles are given at the beginning of any pattern.

Yarn is constructed by twisting strands of fibre around each other. Some yarns are made by twisting three strands, while others are made by twisting four or five strands. One would think that the more strands used the thicker the yarn would be. However, it isn't that simple. The thickness of the strands used makes a difference to the finished thickness of the yarn; this causes some difficulty because there is not a uniform way of labeling either the weight or the thickness of yarns. Each yarn company labels their yarn in a different way. They usually use names to indicate thickness, for example, fingering weight or worsted weight. Most balls of yarn have a band of paper around them, with the size of needles that is most suitable for this yarn written on this band, but it can still be very confusing to find the best yarn and needle size for your pattern. If you are finding it difficult to choose yarn for a project the best thing to do is to take your pattern into the yarn store and ask for help.

Needle sizes are also confusing because there are three different ways of naming different sized needles: the Canadian or British way, the American way and the European or Metric way. We have used the European or Metric way. Pairs of needles have their size printed on their ends. A double pointed needle doesn't have any place to print the size on it so sometimes you don't know what size a needle is. A needle or knitting gauge will help you with this problem. The gauge has a series of holes, starting with smaller and going to larger. You can find the size of a needle by finding the hole that it fits into perfectly. It is great! The gauge lists the three ways of naming the size of needle for each hole. (*Also see page 7* in *A First Book of Knitting for Children*).

## Chart of needle sizes

| European or Metric | 10 | 9 | 8 | 7½ | 7 | 6½ | 6 | 5½ | 5 | 4½ | 4 | 3¾ | 3¼ | 3 | 2¾ | 2¼ | 2 | 1¾ |
|---|---|---|---|---|---|---|---|---|---|---|---|---|---|---|---|---|---|---|
| American | 15 | 13 | 11 | | | 10½ | 10 | 9 | 8 | 7 | 6 | 5 | 3 | | 2 | 1 | 0 | |
| Canadian or British | 000 | 00 | 0 | 1 | 2 | 3 | 4 | 5 | 6 | 7 | 8 | 9 | 10 | 11 | 12 | 13 | 14 | 15 |

# New skills

# Reading a pattern

A pattern will tell you exactly how to make the project illustrated. A good place to buy patterns is in yarn stores. You can purchase either a pattern for one project or a book including many patterns. You must follow the pattern accurately for your project to turn out successfully.

There are usually three sections to a pattern. All the materials that you will need to complete a project are listed in the first section, at the beginning of the pattern. You will find the right sized needles and the right thickness of yarn listed in this section. It is important to follow these guidelines for needle size and yarn thickness.

In this first section you will also find something like this: Tension – 22 sts and 30 rows to 10 cm (4in) measured over stocking stitch using 4 mm (no8/US6) needles. This means that to make the garment in this pattern the right size you must knit to these measurements. Most really good knitters make a trial piece of knitting before they begin and measure it to make sure that they are working to the correct tension. Then they will be sure that the garment will fit. You don't have to worry about this for the patterns in this book.

The second section in a pattern gives the instructions for making the pieces of the project. The instructions are written in a shortened way using abbreviations (symbols or letters) to represent techniques, for example, k = knit. When following a pattern you may need to check the meaning of an abbreviation. There is always a guide to the abbreviations at the beginning of a pattern. Our guide for abbreviations is on page 6 of this book.

Most individual commercial patterns assume that you know how to do the techniques needed to complete a pattern, but we are assuming that you don't know how to do the required techniques. We are including this 'New skills' section to help with any unfamiliar techniques which may arise in the patterns in this book. Remember, if you need to review any of the basic techniques of knitting you could use *A First Book of Knitting For Children.*

## Reading a pattern

In the patterns in this book, one line of instruction usually equals the instructions for making one row (or round). This method of writing instructions takes up quite a bit of space. The instructions in most patterns for experienced knitters are crammed into a smaller space with one line containing instructions for many rows. You are told the beginning of each row of course.

It is a good idea to mark your pattern in pencil as you progress with your knitting so that you will always know where you are in the instructions.

The last section of a pattern shows how to assemble and finish the project. Remember that the success of your finished project will much depend on both the neatness of your knitting and of your sewing up.

# Increasing and decreasing

Sometimes your knitting needs to change shape in width as well as in length. You can add stitches at the beginning of a row or during a row to make your knitting wider. This is called increasing. On the other hand you may wish to make your knitting narrower. This is called decreasing.

## Increasing at the beginning of a row

This is exactly like casting on.
*In through the front door,*
*Dance around the back,*

*Peek through the window,*

*And on jumps Jack.*

15

# Increasing and decreasing

## Increasing in a stitch (inc)

This is almost always done on a knit row. Unlike casting on, this can be done anywhere on the row. This involves making one stitch into two by knitting into the front and the back of the stitch.

*In through the front door, Dance around the back,*

*Peek through the window,*
But leave Jack on.

*Swing needle around.*
*Go in through same Jack's back door,*

*Peek through Jack's back window*

*And off jumps 1 Jack.*
This makes 2 stitches instead of 1.

16

# Make 1 (m1)

This process makes a stitch by using the strand of yarn that lies between 2 stitches of your knitting. In *The First Book of Knitting* we explained how you could accidentally make a hole in your work by knitting this strand. Here we show you how to twist this strand to make a new stitch without making a hole.

Lift the strand of yarn lying between the needles.

Place the strand on the left hand needle.

Take the needle out of the front door of this strand and put it in the back door. This gives the stitch a twist.
Knit as if it were a real stitch.

Can you see the extra stitch on the right hand needle?

17

# Increasing and decreasing

## Decreasing – knitwise (k2tog)

To decrease when you are knitting you knit 2 stitches together (k2tog).
This can be done in any part of the row.

*In through two front doors,*

*Dance around the back,*
*Peek through two windows,*
*And off jump two jacks as one stitch.*

## Decreasing – purlwise (p2tog)

To decrease when you are purling you purl 2 stitches together.
Like k2tog this can be done in any part of the row.

*In through two side doors,*

*Dance around the front,*

*Out through two back windows,
And off jump two jacks* as one stitch.

## Increasing and decreasing

## Pass slipped stitch over (psso)

In our language psso means 'leapfrog' the slipped stitch over the knitted stitch. It is like casting off 1 stitch and then continuing to knit with the remainder.

To slip stitch, take one stitch from the left needle without knitting it.

<u>Knit</u> 1 stitch over to the right hand needle. Pass ('leapfrog') slipped stitch over knitted stitch and off the end of the needle.

# Dividing work to make two or more sections

## Using a stitch holder or safety pin

Sometimes you will need to divide your work into separate sections, for example, in the gnome pattern to make the legs. To do that, some stitches must be put onto a stitch holder or safety pin to rest while you work on the remainder of the stitches. When you have finished working the first section you will put the stitches from the stitch holder or safety pin back onto the needle and then continue to make the second section.

# Dividing work to make two or more sections

## Rejoining yarn

When you have divided your work into sections, have finished one and are ready to start on the other section, there is no yarn for you to work with.  Now you must rejoin the end of the yarn onto the first stitch.

Push end of yarn through the first stitch.
Tie end of yarn to itself.

# Picking up stitches

If you need to add onto a piece of existing knitting you can do this neatly by finding, picking up and knitting stitches along the side or end of the work.

With the right side of the work facing you, find a straight bar of yarn between two bumps on the side or end of the knitting and *dig the needle in* to pick it up.

*Dance around the back* as if it were a real stitch,

*Peek through the window,* and there's the new stitch.

# Ribbing

Ribbing is a combination of knit and purl stitches along the row to create columns and bumps in the work. This makes the work stretchy. It is used on edges of garments, for example, sleeves, hats, tops of socks, to make the garment fit the body better. You can use a variety of combinations of knit stitches and purl stitches to create the rib on your project. Smaller numbers of repeated stitches create better ribbing, for example: k1,p1 – k2,p2 – k1,p2. Remember every time you change the stitch from knit to purl the yarn must be brought between the needles, not over them, to the front of the work. Likewise, when you change the stitch from purl to knit, the yarn must be taken between the needles, not over them, to the back of the work. When working in the round the ribbing can be started on two needles with the work transferred to the round when the ribbing is completed. You can also start the ribbing in the round but it is more difficult. When ribbing in the round make sure that you cast on an even number of stitches on each needle.

# Using different coloured yarns to make patterns

## Hints

These hints refer to working in the round because that is where we have used different coloured yarns to make patterns. The hints are just as useful if you are doing two needle work.

1)   To obtain the best effect, work your pattern after several rounds of solid colour knitting.

2)   If you want your pattern to work out evenly, the number of stitches that make up your pattern must divide evenly into your total number of stitches, for example, for the hat that has 60 stitches in total:        blue(b), white(w)

*this pattern would work out evenly:*        bbwwbbwwbbww

*this pattern would not work out evenly:*        bbbbwwwbbbbwwwbbbbwww

# Using different coloured yarns to make patterns

3) Watch your pattern carefully when changing from needle to needle.

4) When knitting with 2 or more colours, the yarn that is not being used for a stitch is brought along behind the work. This is called 'carrying' the yarn. You need to carry the yarn loosely so that your work does not become tight and puckered.

In this photo you can see the yarn carried on the back of the work and the two colours of yarn being twisted.

5) When knitting with 2 or more colours, the general rule is that after 2 stitches of one colour of yarn all the strands of yarn that you are carrying behind the work must be twisted (tw) around each other before continuing to knit the next stitch. This will keep the carried yarn from making large loops on the wrong side of the work. This technique of 'twist' (tw) is also used to keep holes from developing at the joins when working blocks of colour, for example, when working the owl's face.

# Using different coloured yarns to make patterns

## Creating simple stripes

Changing to different colours whenever you choose can create a randomly multi-coloured, striped hat. Changing at a specific place in each round of knitting will make more ordered stripes.

## Fair Isle Knitting

Fair Isle knitting is *stocking stitch* worked by knitting different coloured stitches to make beautiful multi-coloured patterns.

You may enjoy reading about a young girl who struggled to knit a pair of mitts decorated with a Fair Isle pattern called *over the waves*. This story book is called *Safe Return* by *Catherine Dexter*.

**Simple 2 colour pattern** - for example, for use in making either of the hats, or the slipper socks:

main colour(mc)     contrast colour(cc)

Using main colour(mc) as background, join contrast colour(cc) by tying it onto the main yarn very close to the work.

1$^{st}$ round:  *k1(cc), k1(mc)*, then repeat from * to * to the end of round
2$^{nd}$ round:  k (mc)
3$^{rd}$ round:  *k1(mc), k1(cc)*, then repeat from * to * to the end of round
4$^{th}$ round:  k (mc).

**Dancing men pattern** - for example, for use in making either of the hats, using 60 sts:
1$^{st}$ round: *k1(cc), k3(mc)*, then repeat from * to * to the end of round
2$^{nd}$ round:  k2(cc), k1(mc), **K3(cc), k1(mc)**, then repeat from ** to ** 13 times, k1(cc)
3$^{rd}$ round:  as 1$^{st}$ round
4$^{th}$ round:  solid (mc) knitting to bring out the pattern.

# Using different coloured yarns to make patterns

You could repeat this 'dancing men' pattern using a different contrast colour or you could alternate this pattern with the previous simple 2 colour pattern.  Use your imagination and have fun!

*Simple two colour pattern and dancing men pattern in an unfinished hat.*

# Knitting in the round

Knitting in the round is done with a set of 4 or 5 double pointed needles. You just keep going around and around in a circle. There are two advantages of knitting in this way. The first is that you won't have any seam to sew up. The second advantage is that you can create stocking stitch by knitting every row. Patterns for projects knitted in the round give instructions for rounds instead of rows. A round is the completion of the number of needles that it takes to get back to the same spot in the knitting but one row further on.

Some projects that are knitted in the round, for example the hat with the rolled brim on *page 66*, call for you to cast on with 4 needles. This is a bit tricky. You cast onto the first needle one third of the total number of stitches required. *Then you cast on one more stitch but leave it on the right hand needle, *see photo*. Slide this stitch down to the end of the needle and make it the first stitch of the second needle. Using the third needle, cast one third minus one of the total stitches required, onto the second needle*. Repeat from * to * for the third needle. When you bring the 3 needles into a circle you must be careful not to twist the cast on stitches. The fourth needle is the one you knit with.

This shows the cast on stitch remaining on the right hand needle.

## Knitting in the round

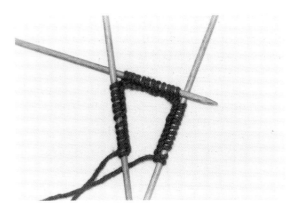

This shows the stitches cast onto three needles, pulled into a circle with no twist between the needles, ready for knitting in the round.

# Turn

In normal knitting one works from the beginning to the end of the row. Stopping in the middle of the row and going in the opposite direction is usually considered wrong. We call this *going the wrong way to market*. But for shaping some projects, for example the heel of the sock, you will need to *go the wrong way to market*. Turn means stop working in the direction you have been working in, turn your work around and work back the other way. The stitches at the end of the row stay on the needle and rest.

# Double casting off

Double casting off closes two edges of your work by casting them off together. This is instead of casting each edge off and then sewing them up. It produces a thinner, neater seam not unlike grafting, but much easier to do.

*Right:* Needles are placed side by side, With the same number of stitches on each. *A third needle goes in through two front doors – first on the front needle, second on the back needle.

*Dance around the back.*
*Peek through two windows.*
*And off jump two Jacks*
*(one from each needle)**
Repeat from * to *.

Then *leapfrog* the two stitches on the Right hand needle.
Continue *jumping off two Jacks* and *leapfrogging* to cast off all the stitches. This photo shows four 'leapfrogs'.

# Making proper holes

Proper holes have two different uses for your work. The first is to provide places for you to thread laces or ribbons through. You will need this for the 'Baby Running Shoes'. The second use of proper holes is to make a lacey effect in decorative patterns. You will use this in the 'Cotton Pop Top'.

Yarn is brought to the front and over the right hand needle.

The next two stitches are knitted together. This photo shows *in through two front doors*.

This photo shows the yarn over the needle making the hole and a new stitch. It also shows the two stitches knitted together, so that the total number of stitches remains the same. You have made a stitch and lost a stitch. The effect of the hole will be more noticeable on the next row when the slipped stitch has been knitted.

# Patterns

Many of the following patterns have been developed and handed down for use in the handwork curriculum of Waldorf schools around the world.  Some of the remaining patterns we have developed ourselves, and some have been adapted from items that have been lent to us or brought for 'show and tell'.

# Pullover Sweater

This Pullover Sweater is made by knitting rectangles with different colours of yarn and will fit an 8 to 10 year old. Any odd balls of yarn may be used provided they are all of the same weight (thickness). The 4 mm needles and 4 ply yarn makes a sweater that is cosy but not too thick.

## Materials

4 x 50 gm balls 4 ply yarn of first colour; 4 x 50 gm balls 4 ply yarn of second colour; oddments of other coloured yarn for decoration (if desired); 1 pr 4 mm needles; sewing up needle or bodkin.

## Working the pieces

Front and back
*First piece*
Cast on 28 sts.
k146 rows (73 wavy lines).
Cast off.
*Make another piece in the same colour.*
*Make 2 more pieces in the other colour.*

**Sleeves**
*First piece*
Cast on 28 sts.
k80 rows (40 wavy lines).
Cast off.
*Make another piece in the same colour.*
*Make 2 more pieces in the other colour.*

Novalla models our pullover sweater.

## To make up

Join two strips of knitting for the front by oversewing the long edges together. You will now press the seam to make it lie flat, by placing the joined strips of knitting with the wrong side up on the ironing board, covering with a damp cloth and pressing with a warm iron. Repeat for the back.

With outer sides facing each other place back and front together. Starting at one edge pin about 10 cms (4 in) along the top to make a shoulder seam. Repeat for the other shoulder seam. This will leave a hole in the centre for your head!

Carefully try the sweater on to check that your head will fit through this hole. Adjust if necessary, then oversew these shoulder seams, and press these seams flat.

Join two strips of knitting for the first sleeve by oversewing the long edges together. Press the seam flat. Repeat for the second sleeve.

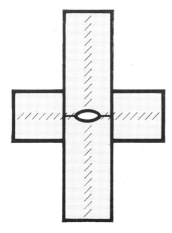

With the wrong sides together, place the joined seam of one sleeve to the joined seam of one shoulder. Pin the top of the sleeve to the side of the front/back piece, then oversew. Repeat with the other sleeve.

Finally, with the right sides together, fold the sweater so that the front and back are together and each sleeve is folded in half lengthwise. Pin from the cuff, up inside the arm and then down the side of the body to the bottom of the sweater. Oversew this seam. Repeat for the other side, then press these seams flat and turn right side out.

Assembly of your sweater is now complete. If you wish, you can do some decorative stitches to cover the seams, or to finish off the neck and sleeve edges.

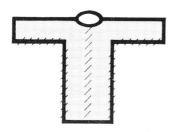

# Gnome

## Materials

150 gm bulky 5 ply yarn (a variety of colours, one of which is suitable for the face and hands), 1 pr 6 mm needles, stitch holder or safety pins, sewing up needle or bodkin, wool fleece or polyester fibrefill for stuffing, leather scrap for pouch.
If you want to make a smaller gnome use 4 mm needles and double knitting yarn.

## Working the pieces

### Body
Using shirt colour cast on 32 sts.
k18 rows for shirt (9 wavy lines).
Change colour for pants. K12 rows.
Next row: k16 and put remainder of sts onto a stitch holder or safety pins.

### First leg
*k12 rows (6 wavy lines).

### Foot
Change colour for boot. Work 4 rows ss.
Cast off*

### Second leg
To begin the other leg slip sts from stitch holder onto needle.
The needle must be facing inwards.
Slip yarn into first st and secure with a knot.
Repeat from * to *.

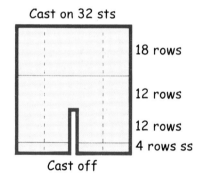

Cast on 32 sts

18 rows

12 rows

12 rows

4 rows ss

Cast off

# Gnome

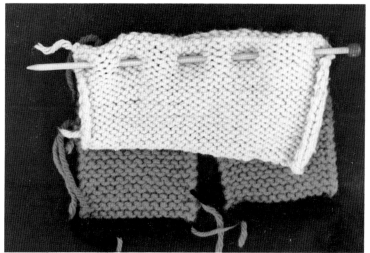

Knitting needle used to pin or 'kebob' the head and body of the Gnome together, before sewing up.

Sammy with the Gnome.

# Gnome

### Head
Using face colour, cast on 28 sts.
Work 20 rows ss.
Cast off.

### Arm
Cast on 10 sts in shirt colour.
k8 rows (4 wavy lines).

### Hand
Change to face colour.
Work 4 rows ss.
Cast off.
Repeat for the second arm.

### Hat
Cast on 32 sts in your choice of colour.
k5 rows.
k2tog at beg. of each row until only 1 st remains.
Cut yarn and pull through loop to finish.

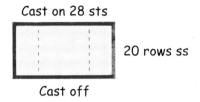

Cast on 28 sts

20 rows ss

Cast off

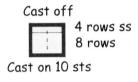

Cast off
4 rows ss
8 rows
Cast on 10 sts

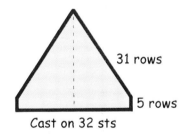

31 rows

5 rows

Cast on 32 sts

## To make up

### To join the body and head
Place the right sides of the body and the head together and 'kebob' using a knitting needle, to ensure the hand and body are joined evenly – *see photo on page 37.*
Using face colour yarn, oversew the seam to join the body and head together.

**Body**

Fold one leg, right sides together. Starting at the boot, sew up the leg using matching colour yarn to make invisible joins. Do the same to the second leg.

Bring the sides of the body together, and sew up along the centre back all the way to the top of the head.

Turn the work through to the right side and stuff the legs, body and head.

Make a circle of stitches around the top of the head, then pull up and secure.

Run a thread in and out of the knitting around the neck. Pull in a little to form the neck and finally secure.

**Hat**

Fold the hat with right sides together and sew from the point down, then turn the right side out.

Fit the hat onto the head of the gnome with the seam of the hat at the back, and pull it down to the base of the neck. Do not stuff. Sew onto head.

**Arms**

Fold the first arm in half lengthwise, right sides together. Sew around the bottom of the hand and up the side seam using matching colour yarn. Turn the right side out and stuff.

Sew the top edges of the arm to the body.

Repeat for the second arm.

**To complete the gnome**

Pinch the face to form a nose and stitch through from one side to the other.

Sew some loops of homespun wool or fleece onto the face to create hair and beard. *See page 36* of *A First Book of Knitting for Children.*

A leather pouch containing a polished rock, some buttons sewn onto his shirt, and some decorative stitching add the finishing touches.

# Gnome

**Leather pouch**

Cut a piece of soft leather like this:

Fold lower edge up to make an envelope:

Punch holes through both pieces together so that they line up. Sew either with thread or make some leather thongs by cutting thin strips of leather, and use these instead of thread.

Cut a strap. Make holes in the ends of the strap and sew onto the first holes on either side of the pouch.

Make 1 hole in the flap. Close the flap and mark where the hole meets on the front of the pouch. At this point make 2 holes in the front of the pouch. Thread a piece of leather in and out of the 2 front pouch holes, then through the hole in the flap for closing.

# Leaping Cat

## Materials

25 gm 4 ply yarn, 1 pr 4 mm needles, stitch holder, tapestry needle for sewing up, gold embroidery thread, embroidery needle, wool fleece or polyester fibrefill for stuffing.

## Working the pieces

### First front leg

Cast on 10 sts.
k30 rows (15 wavy lines).
Slide work to the end of the needle.
Cut the yarn.

### Second front leg

On the same needle as the first leg, cast on 10 sts.
k30 rows (15 wavy lines) .
Finish with both legs on the same needle side by side.
Push them close together to make one piece of knitting.

### Body

Next row: *inc in 1st st, k8, inc in next st*.
Repeat from * to * (24 sts).
The two legs are now joined to form the body.
k22 rows (11 wavy lines).

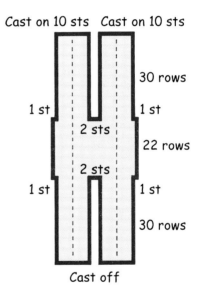

Cast on 10 sts    Cast on 10 sts

30 rows

1 st                    1 st

2 sts

22 rows

2 sts

1 st                    1 st

30 rows

Cast off

# Leaping Cat

First row: k2tog, k8, k2tog (10 sts), put remainder of sts onto a stitch holder.
k30 rows (15 wavy lines).
Cast off.

**Second back leg**
Put sts from the stitch holder onto the knitting needle.  The needle must be facing inwards.
Slip the yarn into the first stitch and secure with a knot.
Next row: k2tog, k8, k2tog (10 sts).
k30 rows (15 wavy lines).
Cast off.

**Head**
Cast on 10 sts.
k16 rows (8 wavy lines) for the back of the head.
Change to ss and work 10 rows for the face.
Cast off.

Cast off

10 rows ss

16 rows

Cast on 10 sts

**Tail**
Cast on 20 sts.
Work 6 rows ss.
Cast off.

Cast off

6 rows ss

Cast on 20 sts

Florian holding the Leaping Cat.

Rabbit under the tree.

# Leaping Cat

## To make up
This project is sewn on the outside, so make sure that your sewing is very neat.

### Body
Fold one leg in half lengthwise and oversew. Repeat for the other 3 legs. Stuff all the legs.
Sew up the body leaving a small opening, then stuff and sew to close up.

### Head
Fold head in half with wrong sides together, then sew up the sides. Stuff.
Go in and out of the loops of the lower edge and pull into a circle, then attach to the body.

### Ears
Pull out one corner of the head. About 1 cm ($\frac{1}{2}$ in) from tip of corner, stitch in and out several times to form and flatten the base and centre of the ear.
Repeat for the second ear.

### Tail
Sew together the casting on and casting off edges of the tail.
Pull this sewing tightly to make the tail curl, and attach to the body.

### Eyes
Use gold embroidery thread to make the eyes.

# Rabbit

The knitting of this little rabbit is very simple – it is just a rectangle, but the sewing up and forming will take some time, and will need experienced and clever fingers!

## Materials

Small ball of 3 ply wool, 1 pr 3 mm needles, tapestry needle for sewing up, wool fleece or polyester fibrefill for stuffing, small piece of fleece for tail.

A larger rabbit can be made using 4 mm needles and double knitting yarn.

A smaller rabbit can be made using skewer needles (*see page 70* in *A First Book of Knitting for Children*) and baby yarn.  You could make a whole family of rabbits!

## Working the piece

Cast on 20 sts.
Knit 60 rows (30 wavy lines).
Cast off.

## To make up

Go in and out of the loops of the cast on edge.
Pull tight to draw the lower edge into a circle. Secure.
Sew two thirds of the way up the side of the knitting. This will form the body and head.
The open third part will form the ears.
Stuff the lower part firmly to make the body.
Stuff the top part lightly to make the head.

# Rabbit

Roll the cast off edge of the knitting in towards the head, to form the ears and the top of the head.

Sew in place at the centre back of the head with 3 or 4 stitches. The ears can remain unsewn.

Decide where the neck should be. Run a thread in and out of the knitting and pull it firmly to form the neck. Secure.

Make a little pom-pom tail from an odd piece of fleece and sew it into place.

Our rabbit, pictured on page 43, is standing up and looking at a special tree.
Your rabbit can also lie down and hide in the grass.

# Sideways Gloves in 3 sizes

Instructions for 3 different sizes are given in this pattern, always in the following order: tot, (junior, adult). Before you start, circle the numbers in the pattern that refer to the size that you wish to make. For example, if you are making the junior size you would circle all the first numbers in the brackets.

## Materials

Small balls of various colours of sport weight yarn (the equivalent of 1 x 50 gm ball for tot, 2 x 50 gm balls for junior, 2 x 50 gm balls for adult), 1 pr 4mm needles, sewing up needle or bodkin.

## Working the pieces

Begin at 'pinky' finger and work in garter stitch.

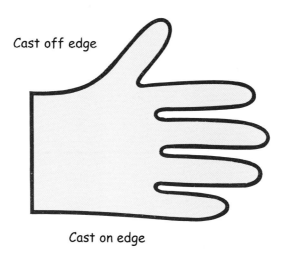

Cast off edge

Cast on edge

# Sideways Gloves in 3 sizes

### 'Pinky' finger
Cast on 24 (30:36) sts.
k6 (6:8) rows.
Cast off 6 (8:10) sts.
For the top side of the first rainbow glove, change colours now (at base of finger).
Continue knitting this row to the wrist edge.
K1 row.

### Ring finger
Cast on 10 (12:16) sts.
k6 (6:8) rows.
Cast off 10 (12:16) sts.
Changing colours as above.
Continue knitting this row to the wrist edge.
K1 row.

### Middle finger
Cast on 12 (14:18) sts.
k6 (6:8) rows.
Cast off 12 (14:18) sts.
Changing colours as above.
Continue knitting this row to the wrist edge.
K1 row.

### Pointer finger
Cast on 10 (12:16) sts.
k6 (6:8) rows.
Cast off 14 (16:20) sts.
Changing colours as above.
Continue knitting this row to the wrist edge.
K1 row.

This special knitting that follows will shape the thumb to the side.

Thumb
Cast on 6 (8:10) sts.
k8 (10:12) sts.  Turn.
k back to the top of the thumb.
k9 (11:13) sts.  Turn.
k back to the top of the thumb.
k10 (12:14) sts.  Turn.
k back to the top of the thumb.
For tot and junior size: cast off all stitches.
For adult size: k15 sts, turn.
k back to the top of the thumb.
Cast off all stitches.

To complete the first glove, make the underside by repeating the instructions for the rainbow glove, but knit in a solid colour.

For the top side of the second rainbow glove, repeat the instructions for the top side of the first glove, but <u>change colours **at the wrist.**</u>
For example, after casting off, having knitted 'pinky' finger, continue knitting this row with the same colour to the wrist edge.
Change colour now, at the wrist end of the glove.
k1 row.

To complete the second glove, make the underside by repeating the instructions for the rainbow glove, but knit in solid colour.

## To make up
Match the pieces together so the outsides are showing, and oversew the pieces together with neat stitches using yarn to match the underside piece.

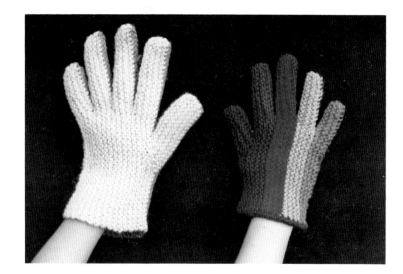

Sideways Gloves.

Theresa launching
her Duck.

50

# Duck

## Materials

50 gm 4 ply yellow yarn, 1 pr $3\frac{1}{4}$ mm needles, stitch holder or large safety pin, tapestry needle for sewing up, orange and brown embroidery thread, embroidery needle, wool fleece or polyester fibrefill for stuffing.

## Working the pieces

Beginning at the underside cast on 16 sts.

1$^{st}$ row: k.

2$^{nd}$ row: *inc in 1$^{st}$ st, k remainder of row*. Repeat from * to * 3 times (20 sts).

### Body with fat wings knitted in

6$^{th}$ row: inc in 1$^{st}$ st, k6, inc in next st, k1, inc in next st, k10 (23 sts).

7$^{th}$ row: k.

8$^{th}$ row: inc in 1$^{st}$ st, k8, inc in next st, k3, inc in next st, k9 (26 sts).

9$^{th}$ row: k.

10$^{th}$ row: inc in 1$^{st}$ st, k10, inc in next st, k5, inc in next st, k8 (29 sts).

11$^{th}$ row: k.

12$^{th}$ row: inc in 1$^{st}$ st, k12, inc in next st, k7, inc in next st, k7 (32 sts).

13$^{th}$ row: k.

14$^{th}$ row: k14, inc in next st, k9, inc in next st, k7 (34 sts).

15$^{th}$ row: k.

16$^{th}$ row: k14, inc in next st, k11, inc in next st, k7 (36 sts).

17$^{th}$ row: k.

18$^{th}$ row: inc in 1$^{st}$ st, k14, inc in next st, k13, inc in next st, k6 (39 sts).

19$^{th}$ row: k.

20$^{th}$ row: inc in 1$^{st}$ st, k14, k2tog, k12, k2tog, k8 (38 sts).

21$^{st}$ row: k.

# Duck

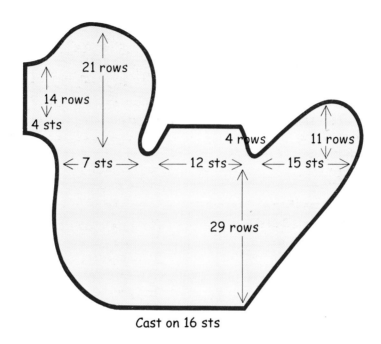

21 rows

14 rows
4 sts

7 sts → ← 12 sts → ← 15 sts →

4 rows

11 rows

29 rows

Cast on 16 sts

$22^{nd}$ row: inc in $1^{st}$ st, k16, k2tog, k9, k2tog, k8 (37 sts).
$23^{rd}$ row: k.
$24^{th}$ row: inc in $1^{st}$ st, k18, k2tog, k6, k2tog, k8 (36 sts).
$25^{th}$ row: k.
$26^{th}$ row: inc in $1^{st}$ st, k20, k2tog, k3, k2tog, k8 (35 sts).
$27^{th}$ row: k.
$28^{th}$ row: inc in $1^{st}$ st, k22, k2tog, k2tog, k8 (34 sts).
$29^{th}$ row: k.

Tail
$1^{st}$ row: k15, put remaining 19 stitches onto the stitch holder or large safety pin.
You will use these 19 sts later to form the top of the back and the head.

You will now continue to work with only the 15 sts closest to the tail end.
2<sup>nd</sup> row: k2tog, k13 (14 sts).
3<sup>rd</sup> row: k2tog, k10, k2tog (12 sts).
4<sup>th</sup> row: k2tog, k10 (11 sts).
5<sup>th</sup> row: k9, k2tog (10 sts).
6<sup>th</sup> row: k2tog, k8 (9 sts).
7<sup>th</sup> row: k7, k2tog (8 sts).
8<sup>th</sup> row: k2tog, k6 (7 sts).
9<sup>th</sup> row: k2tog, k3, k2tog (5 sts).
10<sup>th</sup> row: k2tog, k1, k2tog (3 sts).
11<sup>th</sup> row: k1, k2tog (2 sts). Cast off.

**Top of the back**
Take the 12 sts closest to the tail from the stitch holder, and put them onto a needle.
The needle must be facing the tail.
Rejoin yarn.
k4 rows.
Cast off.

**Head**
Slip the remaining 7 sts from the stitch holder onto a needle.
The needle must be facing the tail.
Rejoin yarn.
1<sup>st</sup> row: k.
2<sup>nd</sup> row: cast on 4 sts, k to the end of the row (11 sts).

3<sup>rd</sup> row: k.
4<sup>th</sup> row: k.
5<sup>th</sup> row: cast on 3, k to end of row (14 sts).
6<sup>th</sup> row: k.
7<sup>th</sup> row: inc in 1<sup>st</sup> st, k to end of row (15 sts).
8<sup>th</sup> row: k.
9<sup>th</sup> row: inc in 1<sup>st</sup> st, k to end of row (16 sts).
10<sup>th</sup> row: k.
11<sup>th</sup> row: inc in 1<sup>st</sup> st, k to end of row (17 sts).
12<sup>th</sup> row: k.
13<sup>th</sup> row: k.
14<sup>th</sup> row: cast off 3, k13 (14 sts).
15<sup>th</sup> row: k2tog, k12 (13 sts).
16<sup>th</sup> row: k2tog, k11 (12 sts).
17<sup>th</sup> row: k2tog, k10 (11 sts).
18<sup>th</sup> row: k2tog, k9 (10 sts).
19<sup>th</sup> row: k2tog, k8 (9 sts).
20<sup>th</sup> row: k2tog, k5, k2tog (7 sts).
21<sup>st</sup> row: k2tog, k3, k2tog (5 sts).
Cast off.

Work a second piece for the other side of the duck.

# Duck

## To make up

### Top of the back
With the right sides together, oversew the top of the back. Leave the sides of the back until you turn the duck the right side out.

### Head
Oversew from the bottom of the back of the neck, over the top of the head to the end of the bill. Leave the front of the bill until you turn your duck the right side out. Oversew from the bottom of the bill, down the front of the body to the corner of the cast on edge.

### Tail
Oversew from where the tail starts at the back, around the end of the tail and down to the other corner of the cast on edge.

Turn the duck the right side out, through the opening between the cast on edges.
Stuff the head, body and tail.
Sew the front side of the top of the back to the bottom of the neck.
Sew the back side of the top of the back to the start of tail.
Shape duck with your hands, adding more fleece if you need to.
Sew up the opening between the cast on edges.

### Bill
Fold the beak so the top seam and the bottom seam are together. The beak should now be lying flat.
Sew the top and bottom of the beak together, going from one side to the other where the beak meets the head. Sew up the end, pulling the corners in to round them.
Use orange embroidery thread to stitch over the bill.

### Eyes
Stitch the eyes with brown embroidery thread.

# Slippers on 2 needles

These slippers are warm and cosy around the ankles.
They are started at the heel and thus can be knitted for a variety of sizes.

## Materials

100 gm bulky yarn, 1 pr 6 mm needles, sewing up needle or bodkin, coat or skirt weight leather for soles.

## Working the pieces

### Starting at the heel

Cast on 36 sts.
1$^{st}$ row: k .
2$^{nd}$ row: k4, p to last 4, k4.
Continue in this way for 16 more rows, or until there are 9 wavy lines at the sides.

### Foot

Cast off 6 sts at the beg. of next 2 rows.
Continue to work in ss until work is the length of the foot.
*For example:* for a 17 cm (7in) foot work 10 rows.
In last row k2tog all across the row.
Cut the thread, leaving it long enough to sew up.  Thread the wool into a large sewing needle and draw through the remaining stitches, pulling tightly.
Fasten securely.

Work the second slipper in similar fashion.

Thread yarn through remaining sts

6 sts     6 sts

ss     18 rows

Cast on 36 sts

Slippers on 2 needles.

Malcolm observing his owl.

## To make up

Turn the slipper inside out.  Oversew the seam on the top of the foot.

Sew the slipper at the back, beginning at the top and finishing half way down the seam.

For the bottom half of this seam sew in and out of the loops of the cast on row.

Pull up so that stitches form a circle for heel, and sew together.

### Sole

Put the slipper onto your foot.

Standing on a piece of leather and using a pen, trace around the slipper to make an outline for the sole.  Cut around this outline.  This makes the sole for one foot.

Flip this first sole over on the leather, and cut out the sole for the second foot.

Use a hole punch to make holes 1 cm ($\frac{1}{2}$ in) apart and .5 cm ($\frac{1}{4}$ in) in from the edge.

Use the same coloured yarn to oversew the sole onto the slipper.

Lily the Lamb
talking to Fiona.

Photo by
David Allerton.

58

# Lily the Lamb

Lily was always the grade I lamb.  She has helped the young children learn how to knit.

## Materials

50 gm 4 ply white yarn, 1 pr 4mm needles, tapestry needle for sewing up, embroidery thread for eyes, embroidery needle, wool fleece or polyester fibrefill for stuffing the head.

## Working the pieces

**Body**
Cast on 26 sts.
Work 10 rows in k1, p1 rib.
Work 28 rows ss.

**Arms**
Cast on 8 sts at beg. of next 2 rows (42 sts).
Work 8 rows ss.  This takes you up to the neck.

**Hole for the neck and the head**
1$^{st}$ row: k19, cast off 4, k to end of row.
2$^{nd}$ row: p to gap in row, turn, cast on 4 sts, turn, p to end of row (42 sts).

**Second side of Lily:**
*This is a continuation of the first side.*
Work 8 rows ss.
Cast off 8 sts at beg. of next 2 rows (26 sts).
Work 28 rows in ss.
Work 10 rows in k1, p1 rib.
Cast off.

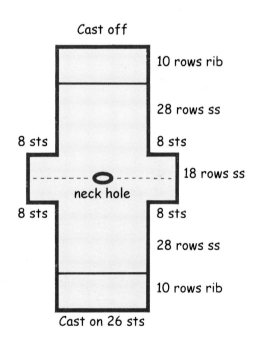

Cast off

10 rows rib

28 rows ss

8 sts          8 sts

neck hole          18 rows ss

8 sts          8 sts

28 rows ss

10 rows rib

Cast on 26 sts

# Lily the Lamb

### Head
Cast on 16 sts.
Work 30 rows in ss.
Cast off.

### Ears
Cast on 7 sts.
Work 8 rows in ss.
k2tog at beg. of every row until 1 st remains.
Cut yarn and thread through st.
Make second ear.

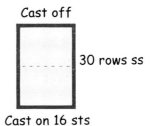

Cast off

30 rows ss

Cast on 16 sts

6 rows ss

8 rows ss

Cast on 7 sts

## To make up

Fold the body in half with the right sides of the knitting together.
Sew around the 'hand', up the 'arm' and down the body to the bottom of the ribbing.  Repeat on the other side.
With the right sides together, fold the head piece in half and sew up the sides.
Turn through to the other side and stuff, leaving enough room for your finger.
Draw the edge of the head into a circle and sew to the edge of the hole in the body.  This is tricky to do, because the edge on the head is longer than the edge on the body, and the former has to be reduced to fit.  To help with this, stick your finger through the hole in the body, and put the head on your finger, then sew the head to the body from the outside with strong stitches.
Sew on the ears to the sides of the head, curling the pointed edges upward.
Finish Lily by sewing some loops of wool on to the top of her head and give her some eyes.

Your Lily is now complete.

It may take a little experimenting to find the hole for your finger in the head stuffing, but once you do, Lily can be brought to life and tell many interesting stories!

60

# Horned Owl

These owls are called 'horned' because of the two tufts of feathers on their heads. Some people think these tufts are horns, while others think they are ears. They are neither horns nor ears. The owl's ears are hidden on the side of the head far below these tufts.

## Materials

50 gm double knitting yarn in grey(gr), 2 small balls of double knitting yarn in beige(be), 1 pr 4½ mm needles, sewing up needle or bodkin, black embroidery thread, embroidery needle, wool fleece or polyester fibrefill for stuffing.

You can make a smaller owl by using 3¼ mm needles and 4 ply yarn.

## Working the pieces

### Body

Cast on 18 sts in grey(gr).

1st row: k.

2nd row: *k3, inc in next st*, repeat from * to * 3 times, k2 (22 sts).

3rd row: k.

4th row: *k3, inc in next st*, repeat from * to * 4 times, k2 (27 sts).

5th row: k.

6th row: **k4, inc in next st**, repeat from ** to ** 4 times, k2 (32 sts).

k 36 rows (22 wavy lines from beginning).

Next row: k to last 8 sts, put these onto a safety pin, turn work.

## Horned Owl

Next row: k to last 8 sts, and put these sts onto another safety pin.
The stitches on the 2 safety pins will be used later for the back of the head.
Work on the centre 16 sts to make the face as follows:
Join first ball of beige(be) yarn onto first stitch.
We suggest you use a second ball of beige yarn, because then you won't have to carry a long thread of beige from the right side of your work over to the left side. You'll see what we mean as you work on the face.

### Face

1$^{st}$ row: k1(be), tw, k14(gr), join the second ball of beige yarn, k1(be).
2$^{nd}$ row: p1(be), k14(gr), p1(be).
3$^{rd}$ row: k2(be), tw, k12(gr), tw, k2(be).
4$^{th}$ row: p2(be), k12(gr), p2(be).
5$^{th}$ row: k3(be), tw, k10(gr), tw, k3(be).
6$^{th}$ row: p3(be), k10(gr), p3(be).
7$^{th}$ row: k4(be), tw, k8(gr), tw, k4(be).
8$^{th}$ row: p4(be), k8(gr), p4(be).
9$^{th}$ row: k5(be), tw, k6(gr), tw, k5(be).
10$^{th}$ row: p5(be), k6(gr), p5(be).
11$^{th}$ row: k6(be), tw, k4(gr), tw, k6(be).
12$^{th}$ row: p6(be), k4(gr), p6(be).
13$^{th}$ row: k7(be), tw, k2(gr), tw, k7(be).
14$^{th}$ row: p7(be), k2(gr), p7(be).
k2 rows (be).
Switch to grey yarn.
17$^{th}$ row: k2tog, k5, k2tog, k5, k2tog (13 sts).
18$^{th}$ row: k.
19$^{th}$ row: k2tog, k9, k2tog (11 sts).
20$^{th}$ row: k.

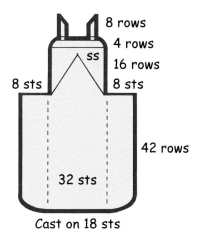

8 rows
4 rows
ss
16 rows
8 sts
8 sts
42 rows
32 sts
Cast on 18 sts

**First feather 'horn'**
1st row: k3, put the remaining stitches onto a stitch holder.
***k4 rows.
6th row: k2tog, k1 (2 sts).
7th row: k.
8th row: k2tog.
Finish last st***.

**Top of the head, and the other feather 'horn'**
Put sts from the stitch holder onto the needle, which should be facing the horn that you have just completed.
Rejoin grey yarn.
1st row: Cast off 5, k3.
Repeat from *** to ***.

**Back of the head**
To make the back of the head, lay the front of the owl face down. Fold the work on the 2 safety pins to meet at the centre. Put the sts from the left hand safety pin onto the knitting needle first, followed by the sts from the right hand needle.
Rejoin the grey yarn.
k20 rows in grey (10 wavy lines).
21st row: k2tog, k5, k2tog, k5, k2tog (13 sts).
22nd row: k.
23rd row: k2tog, k9, k2tog (11 sts).
24th row: k.
Follow the instructions for the *feather horns* for the face section.

# Horned Owl

## Wings
Cast on 32 sts in grey.
k24 rows (12 wavy lines).

## First wing point
1st row: k2tog, k12, k2tog, put the remaining 16 sts onto a stitch holder.
2nd row: k.
3rd row: k2tog, k10, k2tog.
4th row: k
Continue this pattern of k2tog at beg. and end of each <u>alternate</u> row until no sts remain.
Put sts from the stitch holder onto the needle, which must be facing inwards.
To make the second wing point, repeat the instructions for the first wing point.

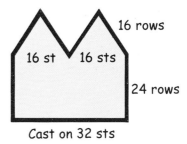

16 rows

16 st    16 sts

24 rows

Cast on 32 sts

## Beak
Cast on 12 sts in beige.
1st row: k.
Working in ss, k2tog at beg. and end of every row until 2 sts remain.
Cast off.
Fold the beak in half lengthwise, with the knit sides together.  Sew from tip to base pulling your stitches tight.

11 rows ss

Cast on 12 sts

64

Turn the beak through to the right side and flatten it with the seam in the middle of the beak, then sew the base together.  The beak should be curved from sewing up.  If you do not feel the shape is quite right you may wish to do some additional sewing.

## To make up

### Head and body
Place the right sides of the front and the back of the head together, then sew across the top of the head between the 'horn tufts'.
Sew down the sides of the head from the bottom of the 'horn tufts'.
Sew the back seam of the body, and turn the whole owl through to the right side.

### Horn tufts
Pull the horn tufts through to the right side.
Join the horn tuft halves together by sewing the centre seam, and then push the side of the head in to meet the bottom of the 'horn tuft' and sew together.
Repeat for the second horn tuft.

### Finishing
Stuff with fleece.
To sew up the bottom, go in and out of the loops of the cast on edge, pull tight and sew.
To create the neck, run the yarn though the stitches, pull tight and secure.
Put wings, with points down, over the owl's shoulders like a shawl, and sew the top edge of each wing to the body.  Finally, attach the wings to the body by sewing from the top down between the wings.
Sew on the beak.
Use a running stitch of dark embroidery thread to outline the eyes.  Our owl is asleep, so its eyes are closed.  If your owl is awake, it will need more black embroidery work in the centre of its eyes.

# Hat with Rolled Brim

This stylish hat is a larger version of the hand doll's hat with rolled brim. You and your doll could have matching hats!

## Materials

50 gm of main colour(mc) 4 ply double knitting yarn, 25 gm of contrasting colours(cc) of similar yarn, 1 set of 5 double pointed 4 mm needles, tapestry needle for sewing up.

## Making the piece

Cast on 100 sts – 25 sts on each of 4 needles *(see pages 28 and 29)*.
Bring into a circle, being careful not to twist the cast on sts. Remember that the start of the round is where your cast on tail of wool is hanging.
k18 rounds for brim which curls up.
k30 rounds for main part of hat, changing colours and inserting patterns when desired.

### Shaping the top of the hat

1st round: 1st needle: k1, *sl1, k1, psso, k6*, repeat from * to * twice more. Repeat the instructions for the 1st needle on the other three needles.
2nd round: k.
3rd round: k.
4th round: 1st needle: k1, **sl1, k1, psso, k5** repeat from ** to ** twice more. Repeat the instructions for the 1st needle on the other three needles.
5th round: k.
6th round: k.
Continue decreasing in this fashion until there are 4 sts remaining on each needle.
Cut the yarn and, using the needle, thread through the stitches, then pull into a circle and secure well.

## To make up

Finish off the ends of the yarn by weaving into the knitting.

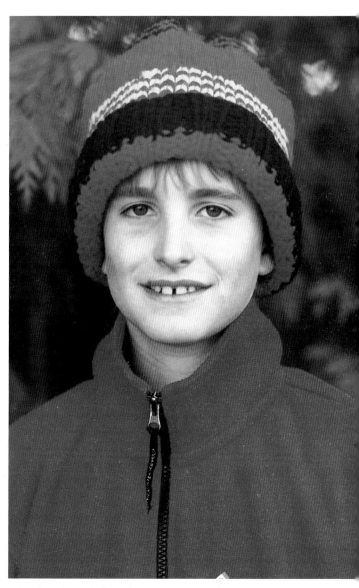

Savannah wearing the hat with the rolled brim.
Photo by David Allerton.

Richard modelling his cosy, warm hat.

# Hat

## Materials

2 x 100 gm balls 5 ply bulky yarn, small amounts of different colours 5 ply bulky yarn for making patterns, 1 pair 6 mm needles for ribbing, 1 set of 5 double pointed 6mm needles, sewing up needle or bodkin.

## Working the piece

You may start knitting this piece using either the pair of needles, or the set of double pointed needles – *see pages 28 and 29.*

Cast on 60 sts.

Work 16 rows (or rounds) in k2, p2 rib.

If you have begun on 2 needles, change to 4 double pointed needles like this:

1st needle: k15, leave needle hanging,

2nd needle: k15, leave needle hanging,

3rd needle: k15, leave needle hanging,

4th needle: k15, draw knitting into a circle.

Now you will be working with your knitting on 4 needles going around in a circle. 1 round is the completion of 4 needles of knitting.

k24 rounds.

### Shaping the top of the hat

1st round: 1st needle: *k1, sl1, k1, psso, k5, sl1, k1, psso, k5*.

Repeat from * to * on each of the other 3 needles.

2nd round: 1st needle: **k1, sl1, k1, psso, k4, sl1, k1, psso, k4**.

Repeat from ** to ** on each of the other 3 needles.

Repeat in this manner, reducing k sts by 1 each time until there are only 3 sts left on each needle.

Cut the yarn leaving a 25 cm (10in) piece.  Using the needle, run this end through all the remaining stitches, draw up and  secure.

## To make up

Sew up the ribbed edge neatly, so that your hat can be worn with either the ribbed edge folded up as a brim, or down over your ears when skiing!

Baby 'Running Shoes'.

Slipper Socks.

# Baby 'Running Shoes'

These 'running shoes' are started on 2 needles. When the sole is finished you pick up the stitches on the two sides and the other end, then work with 5 needles. There is a surprising way of knitting the top of the foot so that no sewing up is needed.

## Materials

25 gm balls of blue(b), green(g), yellow(y) of knitted worsted weight washable yarn, 1 set of 5 double pointed $3\frac{1}{4}$ mm needles, sewing up needle or bodkin.

## Working the pieces

### Sole

Using blue yarn and 2 of the set of needles, cast on 10 sts.

k30 rows (15 wavy lines).

Leave the needle in the knitting.

### Sides of the foot

With a 2nd needle continue with the same yarn, pick up and k14 sts going down the first side.

With a 3rd needle, pick up and k8 sts along the lower end.

With a 4th needle, pick up and k14 sts on the last side.

Now you will be working with your knitting on 4 needles going around in a circle.

Remember, one round is the completion of **4** needles of knitting, which takes you back to the same spot in the knitting, but 1 row further on.

1st round: toe needle: k10,
       1st side needle:  k2, inc in next st, k1, inc in next st, k2, inc in next st, k2, inc in next st, k1, inc in next st, k1 (19sts),
       heel needle:      k3, inc in next st, k1, inc in next st, k2 (10sts),
       2nd side needle: Work as for 1st side needle.

k2 rounds.

Change to (g) yarn.

p3 rounds to create the pattern.

Change to (b) yarn.

# Baby 'Running Shoes'

k3 rounds.
Change to (g) yarn.
p3 rounds.
The next needle, the toe needle, needs 12 sts on it.  To do this, slip 1 unknitted st from the previous needle and 1 from the following needle onto the toe needle (12sts).

## Top of the foot
You are now going to knit using only 2 needles – the toe needle and an empty needle. Continue with green yarn.
At the end of each row in this section leave the last stitch on the needle and slip 1 st from the side needle onto the toe needle, then k or p these last 2 sts together.  Surprise!  This will knit the running shoe closed at the side.
*1st row: k.
2nd row: p.
3rd row: k*.
Repeat from * to * in green.
Repeat 2 times from * to * in blue.
Repeat from * to * in yellow.
This pattern makes 3 rows with the 'bumps' on the same side of the work, so if you lose your place in the pattern you can figure out where you are by looking at the rows of bumps.
Repeat 2nd and 3rd rows of pattern in yellow.
You will now have 41 sts spread over 4 needles.
Spread sts evenly onto 3 needles.

## Ankle
You are now again knitting in a circle, but this time a round is only **3** needles.
1st round: k2tog, k to end of round.
2nd round: a round of holes **k1, wo, k2tog**,  repeat from ** to ** 12 times, k1.
This makes 13 holes.
3rd round: k.

Work 10 rounds in k1, p1 rib.
Cast off.

Repeat for the second shoe.

## To make up

Weave in the ends.
Finger knit a tie about 38 cm (15in) long, then attach a safety pin to the end of it.
With the running shoe facing you, start with the hole to the left centre of the front.
Weave into this hole and out of the next one, and continue in this way until only the last 2 holes remain.
You need one more 'hole' than you made to weave the tie through, so you will now put the tie through the knitting instead of a hole. Gently push the safety pin through the knitting at the corner where the green meets the yellow.
Weave the last 2 holes.

Repeat for the second shoe.

# Slipper Socks in 3 sizes

These slipper socks can be knitted to fit a variety of sizes and foot lengths. Like the sideways gloves, instructions are given in this pattern always in the following order: tot, junior or women, men. Before you start, circle the numbers in the pattern that refer to the size that you wish to make. For example, if you are making the junior or women size you would circle all the first numbers in the brackets.

## Materials

200 gm, (400 gm, 600 gm) 5 ply bulky wool, 1 pr 6 mm needles for ribbing, 1 set of 4 double pointed 6 mm needles, sewing up needle or bodkin, coat or skirt weight leather for soles.

## Working the pieces

Using the pair of needles cast on 28 (32:36) sts, or cast on with your double pointed needles – *see pages 28 and 29.*
Work 10 (16:16) rows in k2, p2 rib.
If necessary, change to 3 double pointed needles like this:
1$^{st}$ needle: k9 (11:12), leave needle hanging,
2$^{nd}$ needle: k9 (11:12), leave needle hanging,
3$^{rd}$ needle: k10 (10:12), leave needle hanging, draw knitting into a circle.
You will now be working with your knitting on 3 needles going around in a circle. One round is the completion of **3** needles of knitting.
k10 (16:16) rounds finishing at the split in the ribbing where a new round begins or at the beginning tail, working a pattern into your knitting if you like.

### Prepare for heel

You work the heel using half of the stitches.
You must now move stitches around a bit. Your next needle needs to have 14 (16:18) stitches on it. Slip some stitches from the following needle to make the right number. Equal up the stitches on the other 2 needles, by slipping some from the fuller to the emptier needle. You will now have one very full needle and two emptier needles.
You will now be doing 2 needle knitting for a while, by using the very full needle, while the knitting on the emptier needles rests.

1<sup>st</sup> row: *k1, sl1, k1, sl1 across row, ending with k2.
2<sup>nd</sup> row: p*.
Repeat from * to * 6 (7:8) times.  There will be 14 (16:18) total rows worked this way.
This forms a rectangular piece of knitting for the back of the heel, and knitted in such a
way to form a thicker texture which wears better.

**Turning the heel**
1<sup>st</sup> row: k9 (11:12), turn (see page 29), p4 (6:6), turn.  5 (5:6) stitches will rest at each side
of your needle.
2<sup>nd</sup> row: k3 (5:5),
> You will now *dry up the 'river', by bringing the banks of the river together.*  The first
> bank is the last stitch of the centre stitches that you have just knitted.  The 'river' is
> the gap that you will see.  The other *bank of the 'river'* is the first of the resting
> stitches.  Go ahead, k2tog, to dry up the 'river'.  Turn.
3<sup>rd</sup> row: p3 (5:5),
> Now *dry up the 'river'* on the other side of the centre stitches by purling 2tog.  Turn.
Continue in this way until the resting stitches on both sides have all disappeared and only
the centre stitches are left.  Knitting this way magically makes the exact shape for the
heel.
Next row: k.

**Picking up the stitches at the side of the heel** - *see page 23*
Now you are preparing to knit in the round again.
Start by using the same needle with the centre sts from the turning of the heel, with the
right side of the work facing you.
1<sup>st</sup> needle: pick up and k8 (10:12) sts at the side of the heel onto this centre needle.  You
are now making the stitches ready for *hiking 'down the mountain'.*
2<sup>nd</sup> needle: on 1 needle k across the 14 (16:18) sts that were resting on **2** needles when the
heel was made.  You are *hiking 'across the meadow'.*
3<sup>rd</sup> needle: with the last needle pick up and k8 (10:12) sts at the other side of the heel.
You are now making the stitches ready for *hiking 'up the mountain'.*

# Slipper Socks in 3 sizes

Now k2 (3:3) sts from the next needle onto this 3<sup>rd</sup> needle to even up the stitches on the two *mountain needles*. You will have 10,10,14 (13,13,16:15,15,18) sts on your 3 needles. This is far too many stitches to make a proper shaped sock so you must reduce them like this:
Next needle: *k to last 2 sts of *'down the mountain needle'*, decrease at bottom by k2tog.
Next needle: k *'across the meadow'* (no decreasing, beautiful, sunny scenery!)
Next needle: at bottom, k2tog at beg of *'up the mountain needle'*, k to end of row*.
Now you are at the *'top of the mountain'*, and enjoy the view. No decreasing here.
Repeat from * to * until the number of stitches on the 2 mountain needles together are the same as the number on the meadow needle.
You will be back to the number of sts that you cast on – tot 7,7,14, junior 8,8,16, man 9,9,18.
Half of the sts are now on 1 needle and the other half are on 2 needles.

## Foot
k without decreasing until the little toe is reached.
Allow for growth if you are knitting for a growing person.

## Toe
1<sup>st</sup> round: *k1, sl1, k1, psso, k to last 3 sts of that side of the sock, k2tog, k1*. Repeat from * to * on the other side of the sock.
2<sup>nd</sup> round: k.
Repeat the decreasing round and the regular round until there are 12 (16:18) sts in total remaining.

**To finish the toe**
Turn the sock inside out by pulling it up through the needles.  Be careful that you don't lose any stitches off the needles – tot 6:3:3, junior 8:4:4, man 9:5:4.
Slip sts from the short needle onto the other short needle.  This will leave all the stitches on 2 needles.
Cast off by knitting through both sets of stitches at once and 'leapfrogging' *(see page 30)*.  We call this 'double casting off'.

## To make up
Weave in the ends of the yarn, and turn the right side out.  Lie the slipper sock flat, and press with a warm iron using a damp cloth.

**Sole**
Put the slipper onto a correct size foot.
Standing on a piece of leather and using a pen, trace around the slipper to make an outline of the sole.  Cut around this outline.  Flip this over and cut out another one.
Use a hole punch to make holes 1 cm ($\frac{1}{2}$ in) apart and .5 cm ($\frac{1}{4}$ in) in from the edge, then use either the same or a contrasting coloured yarn to oversew the sole onto the slippers.

# Cotton Pop Top

*to fit a 5 to 8 year old*

This garment is all made in one piece, beginning at the lower edge of either the back or the front. When made up it can be worn either way round.

## Materials

3 x 50 gm balls sport weight cotton yarn, 1 pr 4 mm needles, tapestry needle for sewing up, 2 large safety pins.

## Working the piece

Cast on 50 sts, leaving about 12" of thread for sewing up.
k2 rows.

**Work 'holey' pattern as follows:**
1st row: k2, yo, k2tog.
2nd row: p.
3rd row: k.
4th row: k.
These 4 rows make the pattern.
Continue until there are 14 rows of holes, and end with 2nd row of pattern.

**Armholes and neck**
1st row: cast off 5 sts, k13, cast off 14 sts, k to end of row.
2nd row: cast off 5 sts, k across the shoulder strap (14 sts).
Put sts for the other shoulder strap onto a safety pin.

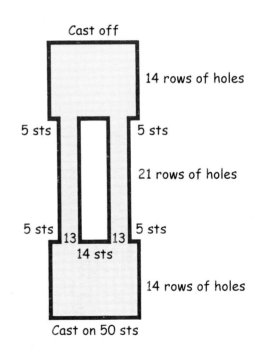

Cast off

14 rows of holes

5 sts      5 sts

21 rows of holes

5 sts      5 sts

13    13

14 sts

14 rows of holes

Cast on 50 sts

Franziska wearing her cotton pop top.

Inuit boy.

79

# Cotton Pop Top

**First shoulder strap**

Work in 'holey' pattern (beg. with 1$^{st}$ row of pattern) and make 21 rows of holes ending with 2$^{nd}$ row of pattern.  Leave these sts on a safety pin.  This shoulder strap is finished.
Cut the yarn, leaving an end for sewing up.

**Second shoulder strap**

Put the sts from the unfinished shoulder strap onto a needle so that the right side of the work is facing you when you begin a new row.
Join the yarn.
Work in 'holey' pattern (beg. with 1$^{st}$ row of pattern) and make 21 rows of holes ending with 2$^{nd}$ row of pattern.

**Second side**

1$^{st}$ row: cast on and k5 sts, k across second shoulder strap, turn, cast on 13sts, turn, transfer sts from the safety pin onto the spare needle, k these sts.
2$^{nd}$ row: cast on and k5 sts, k all across the row (50 sts).
Check carefully because your pattern will not be correct unless there are 50 sts.
Work the second side by continuing in 'holey' pattern (beg. with 1$^{st}$ row pattern).
Make 14 rows of holes ending this side with 4$^{th}$ row of pattern.
Cast off, leaving an end of yarn for sewing up.

## To make up

Weave in the ends of the yarns at the neck edge.
Using beg. and ending lengths of yarn sew up the sides of the garment, securing the last stitches well when finishing.
There is no need to press this top with an iron, but the neck edge does look and fit better if you work 2 rows of single crochet around it.  Perhaps you can either find someone who could teach you how to crochet or maybe a kind friend would do it for you.

# Froggie

Froggie is 'full of beans'. He is fun to play with because he can sit in so many different ways. You will need to sew him up using very small, neat stitches so that his beans won't leak out. He is not suitable for young children because the dried beans could cause injury. Please don't let your froggie jump in the water as the beans will rot if they get wet.

## Materials

50 gm dark green medium weight cotton yarn, a second small ball of dark green medium weight cotton yarn when working the light green stomach patch, small ball of light green cotton yarn for stomach patch and eyes, 1 pr $3\frac{1}{4}$ mm needles, tapestry needle for sewing up, about 200 gm dried kidney beans.

## Working the pieces

### Leg
Starting at the top and finishing at the toe.
With dark green yarn cast on 10 sts.
Work 14 rows ss (beg. with k row).
15th row: k4, k2tog, k4.
16th row: p.
17th row: k4, k2tog, k3 (8 sts).
18th row: p.
19th row: k3, k2tog, k3.
20th row: p.
21st row: k3, k2tog, k2 (6 sts).
22nd row: p.
23rd row: k2, k2tog, k2 (5 sts).
24th row: p.
Work 8 rows ss (beg. with k row).

# Froggie

Sarah holding the green froggie.

## Foot

For help with increasing, *see page 16*.

1<sup>st</sup> row: k1, inc in next st, k2,
   inc in last st (7 sts).

2<sup>nd</sup> row: p.

3<sup>rd</sup> row: k1, inc in next st, k4,
   inc in last st (9 sts).

4<sup>th</sup> row: p.

5<sup>th</sup> row: k1, inc in next st, k6,
   inc in last st (11 sts).

6<sup>th</sup> row: p.

Work 4 rows ss (beg. with k row).

## Outside toe

1<sup>st</sup> row: *k2tog, k2tog, turn.

Leave the remaining 7 sts on the needle for
the other 2 toes.

2<sup>nd</sup> row: p2tog.

Cut the yarn and thread through st*.

## Middle toe

Rejoin yarn.

1<sup>st</sup> row: k1, k2tog, turn.

Leave the remaining 4 sts on the needle for
the last toe.

2<sup>nd</sup> row: p2tog.

Cut the yarn and thread through st.

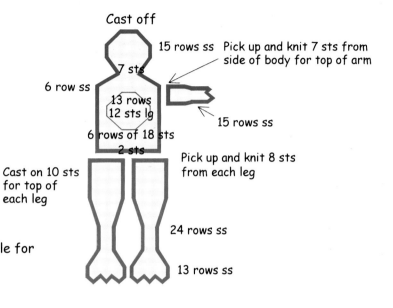

Cast off

15 rows ss  Pick up and knit 7 sts from
   side of body for top of arm

7 sts

6 row ss

13 rows
12 sts lg

15 rows ss

6 rows of 18 sts

2 sts

Cast on 10 sts
for top of
each leg

Pick up and knit 8 sts
from each leg

24 rows ss

13 rows ss

83

# Froggie

**Other outside toe**
Rejoin the yarn.
Repeat from * to *.

Repeat the leg 3 more times.

**Front**
1st row: You now need two leg pieces on which to begin the front. Start at the top of one leg and, with the right side facing you, pick up and k8 sts from the cast on top. With the right side facing you of a second leg and using this same needle, turn, cast on 2, turn back, pick up and k8 from the cast on top of the second leg with the right side out (18 sts total). Now bothlegs will be joined on 1 needle.
2nd row: p.
Work 6 rows ss (beg. with k row).

**Stomach patch of light green:** body – dark green(g), patch – light green(lg).
For help with using different colours, *see page 25.*
Attach the other ball of (g) here.
1st row: k7(g), tw, k4(lg), tw, k7(g).
2nd row: p6(g), tw, p6(lg), tw, p6(g).
3rd row: k5(g), tw, k8(lg), tw, k5(g).
4th row: p4(g), tw, p10(lg), tw, p4(g).
5th row: k3(g), tw, k12(lg), tw, k3(g).
Work 4 rows ss (beg. with p row). Remember to tw.
10th row: p4(g), tw, p10(lg), tw, p4(g).
11th row: k5(g), tw, k8(lg), tw, k5(g).
12th row: p6(g), tw, p6(lg), tw, p6(g).
13th row: k7(g), tw, k4(lg), tw, k7(g). Cut the (lg) and (g) threads.
Use only body dark green now.
Work 3 rows ss (beg. with p row).

### Shoulders
$1^{st}$ row: (k2tog, k2) 4 times, k2tog (13 sts).
$2^{nd}$ row: p2tog, p3, p2tog, p4, p2tog (10 sts).
$3^{rd}$ row: (k2tog, k2) 2 times, k2tog (7 sts).
$4^{th}$ row: p.

### Head
$1^{st}$ row: k1, inc in next st, k4, inc in last st (9 sts).
$2^{nd}$ row: p.
$3^{rd}$ row: k1, inc in next st, k6, inc in last st (11 sts).
$4^{th}$ row: p.
$5^{th}$ row: k1, inc in next st, k8, inc in last st (13 sts).
Work 5 rows ss (beg. with p row).
$11^{th}$ row: k2tog, k9, k2tog (11 sts).
$12^{th}$ row: p.
$13^{th}$ row: (k2tog, k1) 3 times, k2tog (7 sts).
$14^{th}$ row: p.
$15^{th}$ row: k2tog, k3 k2tog (5 sts).
Cast off.

### Back
Starting at the bottom of the body, cast on 18 sts.
Work 20 rows ss (beg. with k row).

### Shoulders
$1^{st}$ row: k2tog, k14, k2tog (16 sts).
$2^{nd}$ row: p.
$3^{rd}$ row: k2tog, k12, k2tog (14 sts).
$4^{th}$ row: p.
$5^{th}$ row: (k2tog, k4) 2 times, k2tog (11 sts).
$6^{th}$ row: p.

# Froggie

7<sup>th</sup> row: (k2tog, k1) 3 times, k2tog (7 sts).
8<sup>th</sup> row: p.

## Head
1<sup>st</sup> row: k1, inc in next st, k4, inc in last st (9 sts).
2<sup>nd</sup> row: p.
3<sup>rd</sup> row: k1, inc in next st, k6, inc in last st (11 sts).
4<sup>th</sup> row: p.
5<sup>th</sup> row: k1, inc in next st, k8, inc in last st (13 sts).
6<sup>th</sup> row: p.

## Eyes:  body – dark green(g),  eyes – light green(lg)
You will be adding stitches in the eye area to make the eyes puffy.
1<sup>st</sup> row: k3(g), tw, (k1, inc in next st)(lg), tw, k3(g), tw, (k1, inc in next st)(lg), tw, k3(g), (15 sts).
2<sup>nd</sup> row: p3(g), tw, (p1, inc in next st, p1)(lg), tw, p3(g), tw, (p2, inc in next st)(lg), tw, p3(g), (17 sts).
3<sup>rd</sup> row: k2(g), tw, (k1, inc in next st, k3)(lg), tw, k3(g), tw, (k4, inc in next st)(lg), tw, k2(g), (19 sts).
4<sup>th</sup> row: p2(g), tw, p6(lg), tw, p3(g), tw, p6(lg), tw, p2(g), (19 sts).
5<sup>th</sup> row: k2tog(g), tw, (k2tog, k2tog, k2tog)(lg), tw, k3(g), tw,  (k2tog, k2tog, k2tog)(lg), tw, k2tog(g), (11 sts).
Use only body green now.
6<sup>th</sup> row: p1, (p2tog, p2tog, p1) 2 times, (7 sts).
7<sup>th</sup> row: k.
8<sup>th</sup> row: p2tog, p3, p2tog, (5 sts).
9<sup>th</sup> row: k.
Cast off.

'Arm'

You will knit the arm straight onto the body.

With the right side facing you, on the side of the front just below the decreases for the shoulders pick up and k7 sts.

Work 7 rows ss (beg. with p row).

8$^{th}$ row: k3, k2tog, k2 (6 sts).

9$^{th}$ row: p.

10$^{th}$row: k2, k2tog, k2 (5 sts).

Work 5 rows ss (beg. with p row).

Smaller 'finger'

1$^{st}$ row: k2tog, turn, leave other 3 sts on the needle for the larger finger.

Cut the yarn and thread through st.

Larger 'finger'

Rejoin yarn.

1$^{st}$ row: k2tog, k1, turn.

2$^{nd}$ row: p2tog.

Cut the yarn and thread through st.

Repeat the instructions for the arm for the other side of the front, except k larger 'finger' first and smaller 'finger' second.

Be careful about the placement of the arm so that it matches the first arm.

Repeat for both sides of the back, making sure the 'arms' are at the same height as the front 'arm' pieces.

# Froggie

## To make up
There are lots of end pieces that you can use for sewing up.  The knit side is the right side.

### Shaping the eyes
It is easier to shape the eyes before sewing the front to the back.
Using green sewing <u>thread</u>, sew all around an eye 2 times.
Pull the thread up tight to make the eye puffy.  Secure the thread.
Repeat for the second eye.

### Legs
With the knit sides together, pin the front leg to the back leg.  Sew down the inside seam, around the toes and up the outside seam.  Turn the legs right side out.
You may need to 'tease' the ends of the toes out with the tapestry needle.
Sew around the ankle then pull tight and secure.
Stitch the front and the back of the flipper together to flatten and shape it.
Repeat for the second leg.

### Head
With the knit sides together, sew from the top of the arm join over the head to the other arm join.

### Arm and the side of the body
Sew from the shoulder down the arm, around the fingers and up the arm to the body.
Sew from the lower arm join down to the bottom of the body.
Repeat for the second arm.
Turn the head and the arms right side out.  You will need to 'tease' the ends of the fingers out with the tapestry needle.
Sew around one wrist then pull tight and secure.
Stitch the front and the back of the 'hands' to flatten and shape.
Fill with dried kidney beans.
Sew up the back/leg seam.

# Inuit Boy

The body, head and hair of the Inuit boy are all worked in 1 piece. His arms are sewn directly onto the jacket. This makes it much easier for him to practice throwing his harpoon!

## Materials

50 gm 4 ply double knitting yarn in red(r), small balls of similar yarn in flesh(f), white(w), dark green(g), black(bl), 1 pr 4 mm needles, 1 extra 4 mm needle, sewing up needle or bodkin, wool fleece or polyester fibrefill for stuffing.

## Working the pieces

### Body
Cast on 32 sts in flesh(f).
Work 26 rows ss.

### Head
1st row: k14, inc in each of the next 4 sts,
   k14 (36 sts). For help here, *see page 16*.
Work 21 rows ss, starting with a purl row.

### Hair
Work 6 rows(bl) ss.
Decrease for the top of the head as follows:
7th row: (k2, k2tog) all across the row.
8th row: p.
Repeat rows 7 and 8 twice more.
Cut the yarn and run it back through sts,
Then pull it up to form a circle and secure.

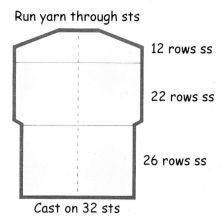

Run yarn through sts

12 rows ss

22 rows ss

26 rows ss

Cast on 32 sts

# Inuit Boy

## Hood

Cast on 60 sts firmly(w).
k6 rows.
Work 2 rows(g) ss,
   (knit, purl).
Work 2 rows(r) ss.
Work 2 rows(g) ss.
Work 20 rows(r) ss.
To cast off k30 sts, fold the
work in half with the wrong
(purl) sides facing out, and
with a 3<sup>rd</sup> needle do double
casting off *(see page 30)*.

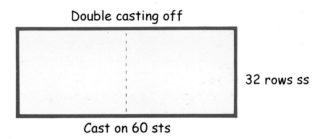

Double casting off

32 rows ss

Cast on 60 sts

## Jacket

Cast on 60 sts firmly(w).
k6 rows.
Work 2 rows(g) ss,
   (knit, purl).
Work 2 rows(r) ss.
Work 2 rows (g) ss.
Work 22 rows(r) ss.
k2tog all across the row.
Cut the yarn, run it back
through the sts and leave it
until later.

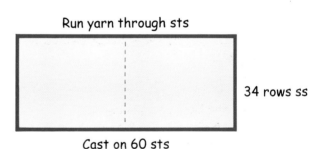

Run yarn through sts

34 rows ss

Cast on 60 sts

**Arm** – *Make 2*
Beginning at the mitten end cast on 18sts(r).
Work 12 rows ss.
k6 rows(w).
Work 2 rows(g) ss.
Work 2 rows(r) ss.
Work 2 rows(g) ss.
Work 4 rows(r) ss.
Decrease for the top of the arm as follows:
*1st row: k2tog, k14, k2tog.
2nd row: p.
3rd row: k.
4th row: p*.
Repeat from * to * 3 times, until only 10 sts remain.
Cast off.

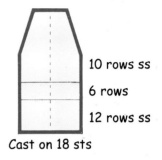

10 rows ss
6 rows
12 rows ss
Cast on 18 sts

**Leg** – *Make 2*
Beginning at the top of the leg cast on 20 sts(g).
Work 16 rows ss.
k6 rows(w).
Work 6 rows(bl) ss.
Increase for the boot as follows:
k7, inc in next 6 sts, k7 (26 sts total).
Work 7 rows ss starting with a purl row.
k2tog all across the row.
p6, fold the work in half with the wrong (purl) sides facing out, and with a third needle do double casting off *(see page 30)*.

Cast on 20 sts

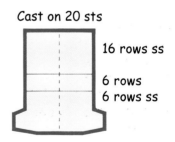

16 rows ss
6 rows
6 rows ss

# Inuit Boy

## To make up

Use appropriate coloured yarn when sewing up.

### Body

With the right sides together fold the body in half lengthwise, and oversew the centre back seam to the top of the head. Turn through to the right side and stuff the head and body.

### Legs

With the right sides together, sew from the boot to the top of the first leg.
Turn through to the right side and stuff.
Repeat for the second leg.

### Joining the legs to the body

Sew the back and the front of the body together at the centre with 3 or 4 sts.
With the leg seam at the back, sew the top of the leg to the body.
Repeat for the second leg.

### Jacket

With the right sides together, sew up the centre back seam.

### Arms

With the right sides together, sew from the mitten end to the underarm.
Turn through to the right side and stuff.
Repeat for the second arm.

### To attach the arm to the jacket

With the right sides out, fold the jacket in half with the seam at the centre back. At the side fold of the jacket, with the arm towards the jacket and the top of the arm at the top of the jacket, sew the cast off edge of the arm to the jacket.

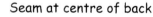
Seam at centre of back

Fold at sides

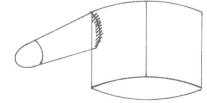

Take the opening of the arm which is close to the jacket and spread it open, then stitch it closed. Repeat for the second arm.

## Hood

With the right sides together, place the centre back seam of the hood to the centre back seam of the jacket.  Sew the cast on edge of the hood to the top of the jacket , from $2\frac{1}{2}$ cm (1in) on each side of the centre seam.

Finger knit 2 x 12 cm (5in) ties in white yarn.

(For finger knitting, see A First Book of Knitting for Children, page  27).

Sew the ends of the ties to the corners of the hood.

## Attaching the jacket to the body

Put the jacket onto the body.  Draw up the yarn at the neck edge and pull it to secure to the body and to form the neck.  Secure.  Sew the jacket securely to the neck all the way round.

## Hair

Make uneven stitches in the black yarn at the edge of the hair.

## Face

Use black yarn to make eyes and red yarn to make a mouth.

# Hand Dolls

These life-like little dolls (21 cm or 8¼ inches high) are very appealing to both children and adults.  Any cotton or cotton and wool blend yarn, which is approximately 4 ply and knits up to a close texture to support the stuffing, using 3 mm needles, would be suitable.  We have even used a fine crochet thread, doubled up.

## Materials

Small balls of medium weight cotton yarn in skin colour and various colours for the shoes, underpants, shirt, trousers, skirt and hat; 1 pr 3 mm needles; tapestry needle for sewing up; wool fleece or polyester fibrefill for stuffing; scraps of yarn or wool fleece for hair and a  button or snap.

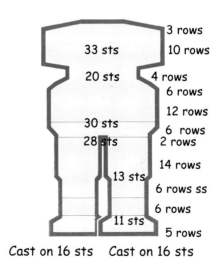

33 sts — 3 rows / 10 rows

20 sts — 4 rows / 6 rows

12 rows

30 sts — 6 rows

28 sts — 2 rows

14 rows

13 sts — 6 rows ss

6 rows

11 sts — 5 rows

Cast on 16 sts    Cast on 16 sts

Nakyta admiring the hand dolls.

# Hand Dolls

## Working the body piece

*Starting with the shoe*
*Cast on 16sts in shoe colour.
Work 5 rows ss (beg. with p row).

| | |
|---|---|
| *For the right leg:* | *For the left leg:* |
| Next row: k4, (k2tog) twice, k8. | k8, (k2tog) twice, k4. |
| Next row: p5, (p2tog) three times, p3 (11 sts). | p3, (p2tog) three times, p5 (11 sts). |
| Change to sock colour. | Change to sock colour. |

### Sock

| | |
|---|---|
| *To make a plain sock:* | *To make a reverse ss sock:* |
| Work 5 rows ss (beg. with k row). | Work 2 rows k. |
| K1 row. | Work 4 rows ss (beg. with p row). |
| Change to skin colour. | Change to skin colour. |

### Right leg
Work 6 rows ss (beg. with k row).
Next row: inc in 1st st and next to last st (13 sts). *See page 16 in the New Skills section.*
Continue in ss for 13 more rows (beg. with p row).
Break the thread leaving an end*, and push the leg to the end of the needle.
Begin the left leg by casting onto the empty needle.

### Left leg
Repeat from * to * remembering to work the foot as written for the left leg.
Push both legs close together on the needle to make one piece of knitting.
Change to underwear colour.

### Underwear
k13 sts from second leg.  k13 sts from first leg (26 sts).
Next row: for girls' underwear, k.  (This will make a frilly edge).
          for boys' underwear, p.  (This will make a plain edge).

**Next row: inc in 1$^{st}$ st and next to last st (28 sts). Next row: p.**
Repeat from ** to ** once (30 sts).
Next row: k.
Next row: p.
Change to skin colour

### Chest and head
Work 12 rows ss (beg. with k row).

### Shoulders:
Next row: k5, (k2tog) twice, k12, (k2tog) twice, k5 (26 sts).
Next row: p.
Next row: k4, (k2tog) three times, k6, (k2tog) three times, k4 (20 sts).
Next row: p.
Work 2 rows ss.

### To shape the head
(k1,m1) 3 times, (k2,m1) 3 times, (k1,m1) twice, (k2,m1) 3 times, (k1,m1) twice, k1 (33 sts).
*For m1 see page 16 in the New Skills section.*
Work 3 rows ss (beg. with p row).

### To make the nose
k16, inc in next st, turn, p2, turn, k2tog, k to the end of the row.
Work 9 rows ss (beg. with p row).

### To shape the top of the head
(k1,k2tog) all across row.
Next row: p.
Next row: k2tog all across row.
Cut the yarn and run through sts, then secure.

# Hand Dolls

**Arms**
Both arms are the same.
Using the skin colour, starting at the shoulder, cast on 6 sts.
1st row: p.
2nd row: inc in 1st and next to last st.
3rd row: p.
Repeat 2nd and 3rd rows 2 more times (12 sts).
Work 10 rows ss (beg. with k row).

**To shape the lower arm**
k2tog at beg. and end of next row (10 sts).
Work 5 rows ss (beg. with p row).
To shape hand
Next row: (k1,k2tog) 3 times, k1 (7 sts).
Next row: p.
Next row: (k1, inc in next st) 3 times, k1 (10 sts).
Next row: p.
Next row: k.
Next row: p2tog all across the row.
Next row: k.
Cut the yarn, run through sts. and secure.
Make the second arm.

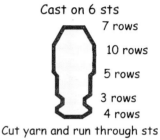

Cast on 6 sts
7 rows
10 rows
5 rows
3 rows
4 rows
Cut yarn and run through sts

## To make up
Use appropriate coloured yarn for the sewing up.
With the right sides together, fold the doll in half lengthwise by folding on the two fold lines.  From the shoe, sew up the inside leg seam.  Repeat for the second leg. Sew up the underwear seam leaving the chest open.
Using the yarn which is threaded through the sts of the head, sew up the head and secure. Turn the right side out.

Stuff the legs. Use little bits of fleece and the flat end of a pencil to push the fleece down to the shoe. Stuff the body and head, then finally the upper body. Close the opening of the chest and sew the edges together neatly on the outside.

Neck

With skin coloured yarn, go in and out around the neck. Pull in a little to form the neck, and secure.

Arms

Fold the arm lengthwise with the right side in. Sew from the hand up to the armpit, then turn the right side out.
Stuff as for the leg.
With the arm seam towards the body and the top of the arm at the shoulder, sew the cast on edge of the arm to the body.
Open the top of the arm and press it flat, close to the body. Stitch in place.

Face

With embroidery thread stitch the eyes and the mouth.
*Hint:* Natural looking features for the face are achieved when the eyes are placed half way down the face. The mouth must be placed so that each eye and the mouth are at the points of a triangle whose sides are all the same length. Make the eyes and mouth look like small dots; this way your doll can be happy or sad.

# Clothes for your doll

You can vary your doll's wardrobe by embroidering designs on the clothes or adding pockets, little buttons, beads or bows.

## Pleated skirt

Cast on 48 sts.
Work 14 rows in k2p2 rib. *See page 24 in the New Skills section.*
Waist
Next row: (k2tog, p2) all across the row.
Next row: (k2tog, p1) all across the row.
Cast off.

## Trousers

*Cast on 23 sts for the right leg.
1$^{st}$ row: k.
2$^{nd}$ row: k.
Work 17 rows ss (beg. with p row)*.
Slide the work to the end of the needle.
For the left leg repeat from * to *.
The two legs should be side by side on one needle, with the right sides facing you ready to begin the next row.
Next row: k across both legs (46 sts total).
Work 11 rows ss (beg. with p row).
Next row: (k1,k2tog) all across the row.
Cast off.
With the right sides together, sew up the centre back seam and both the leg seams.
Turn the right side out.

## Jacket or shirt

This garment can be worn with the opening at the front for a jacket, or with the opening at the back for a shirt.
Cast on 24 sts.

1<sup>st</sup> row: k.
2<sup>nd</sup> row: k.
Work 9 rows ss (beg. with p row).
Sleeves
Cast on 12 sts at beg. of next row, k to end.
Next row: cast on 12 sts, k2, p to last 2 sts, k2 (48 sts).
Work 7 rows ss, remembering to k2 at each end of every p row.

To make the neck
K2, p18, cast off 8 sts knitwise, p17, k2 (40 sts).
Work on each side of the jacket separately now.  The stitches for the second side can stay
on the needle.  Just ignore them!
Next row: *k.
Next row: k1, p to last 2 sts, k2.*
Repeat from * to * once.
Next row: k.
Next row: cast on 6 sts, k6, p18, k2 (26 sts).
Next row: **k.
Next row: k2, p to last 2 sts, k2.**
Repeat from ** to ** twice.
Next row: cast off 12 sts, k to end of row (14 sts).
Work 9 rows ss, remembering to k2 at the neck edge on p rows.
Next row: k.
Cast off.
Rejoin the yarn to the other side of the jacket.
Next row: *k.
Next row: k2, p to last st, k1.* Repeat from * to * once.
Next row: cast on 6 sts, k to end of row.
Next row: **k2, p to last 2 sts, k2.

# Clothes for your doll

Next row: k.** 3
Repeat from ** to ** twice. 4567
Next row: cast off 12 sts purlwise, p to last 2 sts, k2 (14 sts).
Work 9 rows ss (beg. with k row), remembering to k2 at the neck edge on p rows.
Next row: k.
Cast off.

**Pocket**
Cast on 6 sts.
Work 4 rows ss (beg. with p row).
Next row: k.
Cast off.

**To make up jacket or skirt**
With the right sides together, oversew the underarm and sleeve seams.
Weave in odd ends and turn the right side out.  Attach a button or snap, then sew on the pocket.

## Hat with rolled brim

Cast on 35 sts.
Work 17 rows ss (beg. with p row).
Next row: (k1,k2tog) all across row, k2.
Next row: p.
Next row: k2tog all across row.
Cut the yarn, thread through the sts, draw into a circle and secure.
With the right sides together, sew up the centre back.
(The brim will roll up on its own!)

## Hat with knitted brim

Cast on 34 sts.
Work 9 rows ss (beg. with p row).
10th row: (k1,k2tog) all across the row, k1.
11th row: p.
12th row: k2tog all across the row.
Cut the yarn, thread through the sts, draw into a circle and secure.
Do not sew the hat up.

To make the brim
With the right side of the work facing you, rejoin the yarn.
Pick up and knit 33 sts along the cast on edge.
Next row: inc in every st all across the row (66 sts).  This is hard work!
Don't give up.  It gets easier.
k3 rows.
Cast off.
Sew up seam.

## Hair

To make braids, use fluffy wool yarn.
For hair, use strands of woollen yarn or coloured fleece.
Using the same colour yarn as the hair, sew the hair or braids onto the head with big sts.
Put the hat firmly into place.
Using the same yarn as the hat, sew the hat onto the head.
     — for the hat with the rolled brim, sew underneath the part that rolls up.
     — for the hat with the knitted brim, sew just above the brim.

You can use your imagination and skills to make other clothes for your dolls.  For example, your girl doll could wear a plain skirt, and your boy doll might look cool in a muscle shirt — like a simple Cotton Pop Top, *see page 78*.  Be adventurous.  Have fun!

# Biographies

The inspiration for this book came from the students of the Vancouver Waldorf School. For them, completion of a handwork project always brings joy and great satisfaction.

Jill Allerton is in the early stages of retirement, filling her days with all those activities that earlier she had to squeeze into her non-teaching hours. She can now play much more tennis, knit and sew and cook and read and spend much more time with her grandchildren. And she does!

Bonnie Gosse loves teaching soapstone carving to students of all ages. Teaching English to Japanese 'seniors' is an exciting new endeavour in her life. She finds their wisdom and enthusiasm to be life long learners an inspiration.

Jill and Bonnie have together written *A First Book of Knitting for Children*.

Bonnie                                    Jill

# A First Book of Knitting for Children

## Bonnie Gosse and Jill Allerton

*With photography by Dave Gosse and Bryan Anderson.*

This is a knitting book with a difference. Rhymes and photos show in detail the basic steps of knitting. A thorough introduction to knit stitch and purl stitch is followed by simple, enticing patterns for animals. The patterns are easy and exciting to make and the completed projects are fun to play with. Although written for children, this book is a valuable resource for adults. Handwork teachers, parents and grown-ups wishing to learn how to knit will find that the simple to follow instructions, the interesting patterns and the artistic photographs make this book a must for their collection.

*72 pages. Size 197 x 210 mm. Sewn paperback with colour illustrated cover.*
*12 full colour illustrations and numerous black and white photographs.*
*Published by* **Wynstones Press**. *ISBN 0 946206 36 8.*

# Wynstones Press

**Wynstones Press** publishes a range of books, mostly for children, parents and teachers. These include childrens' picture books, childrens' fiction and resource books.
The resource books cover a variety of subject areas, including knitting, poems, songs and stories for young children, pentatonic music and a volume on ancient mythologies.

Also available is a wide selection of postcards, folded cards and prints reproduced from original work by a variety of different artists.

**Wynstones Press** distributes a selection of Advent Calendars.

For further information please contact:

**Wynstones Press**
Ruskin Glass Centre
Wollaston Road
Stourbridge DY8 4HF. England.

Telephone: +44 (0) 1384 399455.
Email: info@wynstonespress.com
Website: wynstonespress.com

# Knitting for Children

Published by:

**Wynstones Press**
Ruskin Glass Centre,
Wollaston Road, Stourbridge,
West Midlands DY8 4HF. England.
Telephone: +44 (0) 1384 399455.
Email: info@wynstonespress.com
Website: wynstonespress.com

First Edition 2002.

Typeset and printed by Wynstones Press.

British Library Cataloguing-in-Publication Data:
A catalogue record for this book is available from the
British Library.

ISBN 0 946206 53 8